PANDAS

A PORTRAIT OF THE ANIMAL WORLD

Jill Caravan

TODTRI

This book was designed and produced by
Todtri Productions Limited
P.O. Box 572
New York, NY 10116-0572
Fax: (212) 279-1241

Printed and bound in Singapore

ISBN 1-880908-66-2

Author: Jill Caravan

Publisher: Robert Tod
Book Designer: Mark Weinberg
Production Coordinator: Heather Weigel
Senior Editor: Edward Douglas
Project Editor: Cynthia Sternau
Assistant Editor: Linda Greer
DTP Associate: Michael Walther
Typesetting: Command-O, NYC

PHOTO CREDITS
Photographer/Page Number

Peter Arnold, Inc.
Pu Tao 8-9, 23 (bottom), 54, 56-57

Tom and Pat Leeson 3, 14, 17 (bottom), 18, 24-25, 26, 27 (top & bottom), 29, 33, 34, 36, 37, 38 (top),
39, 41 (top & bottom), 42 (top & bottom), 43, 45 (top), 48-49, 50, 51, 52 (top), 53, 57 (right), 58

National Geographic Society
Pat Wenshi 7 (top), 17 (top), 28, 30, 31 (top & bottom), 32, 60 (top & bottom), 61, 64-65, 68-69, 70
Lu Zhi 4, 5, 6, 7 (bottom), 10 (bottom), 11 (bottom), 16, 19, 20, 21, 23 (top), 35, 38 (bottom),
40, 45 (bottom), 46, 47, 52 (bottom), 59, 62, 63 (top & bottom), 66 (top & bottom), 67, 71

Photo Researchers, Inc.
Tim Davis 55

Picture Perfect USA
E. R. Degginger 12
Stephen Kirkpatrick 13 (top)
John Warden 13 (bottom)

The Wildlife Collection
Martin Harvey 10 (top), 11 (bottom), 15, 44
Dean Lee 22

INTRODUCTION

The appeal of the giant panda is quite far-reaching, especially considering that there is very little chance of the average person in most parts of the world actually ever seeing one.

Just about everyone is familiar with the panda. We've all seen them in toy stores or in children's rooms, among rows and rows of the ever-popular teddy bear and other stuffed animals. Pandas are abundant on T-shirts, on posters, in pictures, on greeting cards, on hats, as cartoon characters, and even as the symbol for a worldwide wildlife organization.

The panda's appeal is quite far reaching, especially considering that there is very little chance of the average person in most parts of the world ever setting eyes on one. With other animals whose range does not extend into your own backyard, you can expect to find them at your local zoo. But this is not the case with the panda. There are only a handful of zoos around the world at which onlookers can spend time observing a panda through the glass or railed wall of an enclosure.

The panda is among the world's most endangered species. As the twentieth century draws to a close, the world's various wildlife conservation organizations collectively estimate that there are not more than one thousand pandas still in existence. Most of these remaining bears roam the bamboo forests of western and southwestern China, and about one hundred are in captivity, mainly in their native China. Only nine live in zoos outside China, and only one of those lives in the United States—a male named Hsing-Hsing, at the National Zoo in Washington, D.C. Why then does a picture or any other image of a panda evoke a smile on people's faces? What is it about this isolated, unobtrusive, apparently content animal that brings out such joy in people?

Like any "teddy bear," it displays many of the same qualities of the human baby—those that nature has provided to bring out maternal and paternal instincts: a large head, which sometimes appears as though it will at any moment wobble off its base; a flat face, in comparison to that of most animals of the world, which gives it a more human look; the appearance of large, wide eyes, which suggest a childlike quality; and a rounded body outline, a feature of most mammals, which are generally more appealing to humans than other animals such as reptiles.

The unaggressive giant panda is usually pictured lying on a branch or slouching against a cage or tree, looking as though it has just woken from a nap or is digesting a large meal.

The giant panda's black-and-white coloring is certainly distinctive and seems to have a special appeal to humans both young and old.

THE GENTLE GIANT

The panda also has a reputation as a "gentle giant," in that it appears to be extremely clumsy and lumbering, calm, and innocent, and is rarely depicted as aggressive or violent. In fact, pandas are usually pictured lying on a branch or slouching against a cage or tree, looking quite casual and relaxed as though they have just woken from a nap or are still digesting a large meal. An additional and especially charming feature is the panda's distinct black-and-white coloring, a contrast that is eye-catching and seems to have a special allure for humans.

On all fours, nose to back end, the adult panda is 4 to 6 feet long (1.2 to 1.8 meters) and can weigh up to 350 pounds (160 kilograms). The average panda is 5 feet long (1.5 meters) and more than 200 pounds (90 kilograms)—about the same size as the American black bear.

Its coat is thick and woolly, mainly white, with black on the legs, around its neck, on its ears and as eye patches on its face. Brown pandas have been known to exist, although the number of these has been no more than that which a human can count on his or her fingers. Because some mammals are brown at birth and change color, researchers have speculated that brown could be the panda's true ancestral color, occasionally revealed by a recessive gene.

The panda has a stubby tail and, unlike other bears, its pupils have vertical slits like those of the cat. It also has a distinctive skull, which reflects its adaptation to herbivory: The enlarged cranium provides extra grinding power and strong teeth for crushing bamboo.

It has unique front paws—one of the wrist bones is enlarged and elongated and is used like a thumb, enabling the panda to grasp and strip leaves from the stalks of bamboo. Although it is rather nearsighted, its senses of

This lone giant panda, sitting on a hillside in Quinling, China, is obliviously chewing on bamboo leaves, unaware that it is among an elite group of only about one thousand of its species still in existence.

The giant panda's persona is that of a "gentle giant," in that it appears to be extremely clumsy and lumbering, calm, and innocent, and is rarely depicted as aggressive or violent.

Hugging the tree, giant pandas inch themselves upward a bit at a time, in caterpillar-like movements. Descent is usually managed backwards, tail first, in the same manner.

Following page: Giant pandas are less adept at climbing than other bears, and getting way out on a limb like this is not necessarily a smooth operation. They usually retreat upward when threatened by wild dogs or other predators.

In contrast to the giant panda's length of 4 to 6 feet (1.2 to 1.8 meters) and weight of up to 350 pounds (160 kilograms), the lesser panda is only 20 to 24 inches long (50 to 61 centimeters) from nose to behind and weighs 7 to 10 pounds (3 to 4.5 kilograms).

While the giant panda is generally thought of as a cuddly, gentle creature, the configuration of its teeth shows it to be a predator capable of supplying any part of its omnivorous diet.

smell and hearing are powerful enough to see it through most of its activities.

Unlike other bears, the panda does not walk upright on its hind legs. Sometimes, however, it heaves itself up to a standing position against a vertical object and, like an ape or a human, it is able to sit upright, usually leaning against something.

Its walk is decidedly bear-like, called the "diagonal walk," a sort of rolling gait, or waddling, with rotation of the shoulders and hips. Its stride is a bit longer than most bears, head down below shoulders and tail down close against the body. It usually walks along at a leisurely pace, and might sometimes walk a bit faster, at sort of a racewalking trot. But unlike other bears, it rarely sees the need to gallop, even in stressful situations.

Pandas are also less adept at climbing than their woolly counterparts. Although they are frequently pictured in trees, and usually retreat there when threatened, such as by wild dogs, getting up the tree is not usually a smooth operation. They seem to hug it and inch themselves up a bit at a time, in caterpillar-like movements. Unless the panda can return

down by walking along the branch, it descends backward, tail first, in the same manner.

The panda's persona is that of a meek, silent animal, but it is capable of producing a variety of sounds: bleating, chirping, huffing, snorting, and even "barking" when unnerved. And, if given the chance, the panda is able to inflict serious wounds. A few in zoos have even been known to maul their keepers by swiping out with a paw, thrusting forward or pulling a victim towards themselves and then biting.

The long, ringed tail of the lesser panda makes it look like a brighter version of its raccoon relative. Its soft, rust-colored coat is marked with black on the face and ears and with white over the eyes and on the tips of the ears.

One of the giant panda's wrist bones is enlarged and elongated, and is used like a thumb, enabling it easily to grasp and strip leaves from the stalks of bamboo plants.

Bear or Raccoon?

Only a few other animals sport extraordinary black-and-white differentiation like the panda's—the zebra, the penguin, the skunk, the raccoon. That the raccoon is one of the other animals designated with this stark, sectional contrast may be what originally lent credence to the belief that the panda is a member of the raccoon family.

The giant panda, the one we are all used to seeing in print and on film, is technically classified as a bear (*Ailuropoda melanoleuca*, the only member of the genus *Ailuropoda*). Another East Asian animal considered to be related to the giant panda, the lesser panda (also called the red or common panda), is, however, a member of the raccoon family (*A. fulgens*, the sole member of the genus *Ailurus*).

While most of us have always considered the giant panda a bear, scientists have made

A fierce brown bear, Ursus arctos, bares its teeth in a snarling roar. The pronounced canines of the brown bear are very similar to those of the gentle giant panda.

Although the giant panda walks much like other bears— such as this grizzly bear eating salmon—using a rolling gait called a "diagonal walk," it usually takes a much more leisurely pace.

The raccoon and the lesser panda are related. The giant panda's black-and-white differentiation was perhaps one of the reasons it was once believed to be a member of the raccoon family.

an issue over the years of whether it *is* actually a bear. Although its overall appearance seems bear-like, its specialized diet led some people to conclude that it was related to the bamboo-eating red panda. But now, blood protein tests have led scientists to conclude that it is a member of the bear family.

The lesser panda is only 20 to 24 inches long (50 to 61 centimeters) from nose to behind, and weighs 7 to 10 pounds (3 to 4.5 kilograms). Because of its cat-like appearance, it is sometimes called a "bear cat" or "cat bear." It has a bushy, ringed tail from 11 to 19 inches long (28 to 48 centimeters); its long, soft coat is mostly rust, with black markings on its face and ears and white spots over the eyes and on the tips of the ears.

One of the giant panda's unique features is that it is the only species outside the apes known to have a functional opposable thumb. The two types of thumb are strictly analogous to their functions; the giant panda thumb, unlike the primate thumb (which is a modified fifth digit), is an extension of the radial sesamoid wrist bone and functions as a sixth digit, enabling the giant panda to strip the leaves from bamboo stalks with considerable dexterity. This characteristic is among those that have confused taxonomists on the bear/raccoon issue.

Whereas alpine bears generally hibernate, the giant panda does not. (Bamboo is thought to provide insufficient fuel for hibernation.) The giant panda does not growl or roar like a bear, but bleats more like a sheep. In addition, on a cellular level, biologists have been perplexed by the fact that, in both number and morphology, its twenty-one pairs of chromosomes more closely resemble those of the red panda (which has twenty-two pairs) than they do those of bears (with thirty-seven pairs).

Looking closely at the cat-like face of this lesser panda, it is easy to imagine why it is sometimes called a "bear cat," or "cat bear."

The lesser panda, a relative of the giant panda and the raccoon, is also called the red or common panda, and is the sole member of the genus Ailurus (A. fulgens).

ORIGIN OF THE GIANT PANDA

The giant panda's current state of affairs—extremely endangered—is not a very fitting conclusion to a history that is thought have begun more than 600,000 years ago. Some experts say pandas existed even earlier, three million years before the anthropoid apes evolved into *homo sapiens* (humans), in what is now southern China's tropical and subtropical jungles.

Approximately 600,000 to 750,000 years ago, during the Pleistocene Era, the giant panda started to increase its range northward into the Qinling Mountains, and its population peaked. Because of the increase in population, the giant panda also evolved into a larger animal, averaging about twelve percent larger than its current height of 4 to 5 feet (1.2 to 1.5 meters). As the panda population spread, they adapted to the mild and cool climate of the northern forests, as well as to the tropical and subtropical jungles of the south; fossil remains have been found in present-day Burma.

And life was good for several hundred-thousand years, until approximately 18,000 years ago, when the Ice Age began. The northern inhabitants were swept out of existence, and those in the south were greatly reduced. An even larger setback came from the human race in the past few hundred years.

As the giant panda spread throughout China, it adapted to the mild and cool climate of the northern forests, as well as to the tropical and subtropical jungles of the south.

The world of a giant panda consists of areas like this one: The fertile peaks of the Qionglai Mountains along the Zheng River in what is now the Wolong Nature Reserve in China.

Some of the earliest writings on the giant panda called this famous black-and-white bear, first "discovered" by the Western world in China in 1869, "an interesting novelty for science."

The Hunt Begins

Europe first became familiar with the giant panda in 1869, when a French missionary named Père Armand David went to the mountainous country of China's Sichuan Province to search for rare plant and animal life.

The very first mention of the giant panda comes under Père David's entry in his diary for March 11, 1869:

> On returning from our excursion we are invited to rest at the home of a certain Li, the principal landowner in the valley, who entertains us with tea and sweetmeats. At this pagan's I see a fine skin of the famous white and black bear (*du fameux ours blanc et noir*), which appears to be fairly large.
>
> It is a very remarkable species and I rejoice when I hear my hunters say that I shall certainly obtain the animal within a short time. They tell me that they will go out as early as tomorrow to kill this carnivore which it seems must constitute an interesting novelty for science.

On March 23 he wrote:

> My Christian hunters return today after a 10-day absence. They bring me a young white bear, which they took alive but unfortunately killed so it could be carried more easily. The young white bear, which they sell to me very dearly, is all white except the four limbs, ears, and around the eyes, which are deep black. The colors are the same as those of the adult's skin which I examined the other day at the home of Li, the hunter. This, therefore, must be a new species of *Ursus*, which is very remarkable and not only for its color, but also because of its paws which are hairy underneath, and for other characters.

On April 1, he felt it had been confirmed that the animal must be a new species:

> They bring me a white bear which they tell me is fully adult. Its colors are exactly the same as those of the one young that I have already, only the black is less pure and the white more soiled. The animal's head is very big and the muzzle round and short instead of being pointed as in the Pekin bear.

Père David named the animal *Ursus melanoleucus* ("black-and-white bear") and sent a description of it to Professor Alphonse Milne-Edwards in France :

> *Ursus melanoleucus* . . . Very large according to my hunters. Ears short. Tail very short. Hair fairly short; beneath the four feet very hairy. Colors: white, with the ears, the surroundings of the eyes, the tip of the tail and the four legs brownish-black. The black on the forelegs is joined over the back in a straight band. I have just received a young bear of this kind and I have seen the mutilated skins of adult specimens. The colors are always the same and equally distributed. I have not seen this species, which is easily the prettiest kind of animal I know, in the museums of Europe. Is it possible that it is new to science?

When Père David's specimens reached Paris, Milne-Edwards examined the skins and skeletons and concluded that David had been

Europe first became familiar with the giant panda in 1869, when a French missionary, Père Armand David, went to the mountainous country of Sichuan Province to search for rare plant and animal life.

The beautiful natural landscape of China is where giant pandas began their existence—some experts say 600,000 years ago, others claim it was more than three million years in the past.

wrong in identifying the creature as a bear. Milne-Edwards said, although its external form resembles a bear, its "osteological characters and the dental system clearly distinguish it from the bears and come nearer to the pandas and raccoons." When he said "panda," he was referring to the resemblance between the feet of the new animal and those of the lesser panda (*Ailurus*), the only animal then known as the panda.

He began identifying it as the genus *Ailuropoda*, but modified it to *Ailuropus* because of the resemblance to the lesser panda. During the nineteenth century, it became known as *Ailuropus melanoleucus* ("panda-like black-and-white animal"). Later scientists changed it back to Milne-Edwards' original suggestion, *Ailuropoda melanoleuca*, meaning "black-and-white panda-foot."

The word "panda" comes from the country of Nepal, which lies south in the Himalayan Mountains, and means "bamboo eater." When Westerners "discovered" the lesser panda, they adopted the native name for it.

Despite all the names the giant panda has been given in China—"cat bear" (hsiung-maou), "white bear" (bei-shung or pei-shung), "speckled bear" (hua-hsiung), and "monk bear" (ho shien)— it has never been well known in there. So it was relatively safe from human predators, until Western expeditions began coming to the wilderness to hunt this strange animal.

The first Western hunters to shoot a giant panda were the Roosevelt brothers, Theodore and Kermit, sons of American president Theodore Roosevelt, on April 13, 1929, at Yehli Sikang Province, during the Kelley-Roosevelt expedition. The skin of their fully grown male giant panda was sent back to the United States with another specimen which the expedition obtained from local hunters. These were mounted and displayed in Chicago's Field Museum, starting a demand for such giant panda mountings.

Eventually, giant panda specimens were acquired for the Philadelphia Natural History Museum, the Shanghai Museum, the

American Museum of Natural History in New York, and the National Museum in Washington, D.C. Between 1929 and 1942, one giant panda purveyor obtained fifteen skins and skeletons for the museum in Washington.

Hunters eventually figured out that it was to their advantage to scan the trees looking for sleeping or sunbathing giant pandas, rather than looking on the ground where they would be camouflaged by jungles of bamboo and rhododendron.

During this century, the giant panda's home— the forest area of China—has been disappearing rapidly because of logging, population growth, and agricultural expansion. Barely twelve percent of China's land remains as forest, the lowest proportion of any major country in the world.

With its teddy-bear-like appearance, it is ironic to consider that the first giant panda to be shot by Westerners was felled by the sons of Theodore "Teddy" Roosevelt, who originally named the teddy bear.

Because not much was known about the care of giant pandas, this modern-day giant panda in captivity receives much better care than those captured during the giant panda craze of the 1930s.

Giant Pandas in Captivity

By 1934, William Harvest Harkness, Jr. was making preparations to provide the Bronx Zoo with a living giant panda. His expedition reached Shanghai in January of 1935, and eventually he became the only member of his party. In February of 1936 William Harkness was found dead in Shanghai, apparently having never discovered the giant panda.

His widow, Ruth, whom he had married just weeks before his departure for China, picked up where he left off. She was aided by Jack Young, a famous, American-born Chinese hunter; his brother, Quentin; and

several other local hunters.

Eventually the group came upon a baby giant panda, whimpering inside an old dead tree. It weighed only 3 pounds (1.35 kilograms) and was so young (approximately ten days) that its eyes were still closed. When Harkness later wrote about holding it in her arms for the first time, she said, "That little black-and-white ball nuzzled my jacket, and suddenly, with the sureness of age-old instinct, went straight to my breast."

Quentin carried it back to camp, where it was fed from a bottle. Harkness named it Su Lin, after Young's wife, translated as "little bit of something very cute."

When giant pandas were first hunted by men with guns, they were easy prey because they did not feel threatened by a danger they knew nothing of. Now, eagerly sought by researchers and photographers, they have adapted to that "threat" and are quite difficult to spot.

Like many mammals, the giant panda is active in the morning and again in the evening, with a sleep or rest period mid-day and in the middle of the night. Giant pandas in zoos spend the morning patrolling and cleaning themselves.

Following page: Many giant pandas, captured when they were still cubs, were mistakenly identified as the wrong gender. As is apparent in this photo, the panda has no outstanding characteristics in the genital area.

Although it does not always look like a tree will support a giant panda, this one seems to be very comfortable in the tree nook, gazing down at its surroundings.

There is no way to tell if this giant panda is a male or a female, and panda sexes were commonly mistaken in the early days of giant panda capture and captivity.

In China the giant panda has been known by many names, including "cat bear" (hsiung-maou), "white bear" (bei-shung or pei-shung), "speckled bear" (hua-hsiung), and "monk bear" (ho shien).

Su Lin

The baby panda was taken back to Chengtu, where special arrangements were made for it to travel to Shanghai by air. At Shanghai Airport, the little woven bamboo basket containing Su Lin was rushed to a waiting car to avoid the crowd of newspaper photographers and reporters.

Some accounts say that William Tangier Smith, a colleague and then a rival of the original Harkness group, actually was the first person to capture a live giant panda. But even if that is true, his giant pandas never made it out of the country, so Harkness' widow remains the first to export a live giant panda. The infant, thought to be female, arrived in San Francisco on December 18, 1936. Harkness had brought back bamboo shoot specimens for scientists to use to develop a substitute on which to wean Su Lin when the time came. Considering the legality and safety of allowing the foreign plants in the country, the United States Department of Agriculture held up the giant panda's departure from California. Eventually the agency allowed the bamboo to enter the country, as long as all dirt was washed from the roots.

The giant panda was transported across the country by train, passing through Chicago, and eventually arriving in New York on December 23. Throughout her trip across the country and during her stay in New York, Su Lin became a giant panda ambassador of sorts, swaying most of the world against the idea of hunting down the endearing creatures and killing them. Even the Roosevelt brothers, known for being the first Westerners to kill one, reversed their stand.

Although intended from the start as the depository for the now-famous giant panda, the Bronx Zoo in New York was hesitant about officially acquiring Su Lin, expressing some concerns about its health and future. So Harkness returned to Chicago with Su Lin, who was deposited at the Brookfield Zoo on February 8, 1937. She was formally acquired there in April, becoming the first zoo-owned giant panda, and died April 1, 1938, of food obstruction. She was the first of very few giant pandas to be exhibited in the West.

Brown giant pandas such as this one are very rare, but they do exist in the wild. Because some mammals are born brown and change color, researchers have speculated that brown could be the giant panda's true ancestral color.

The word "panda" comes from Nepal, where it means "bamboo eater." The giant panda was given its name—actually the native name of the lesser panda—by the Westerners who first "discovered" it.

Finding a Mate

Harkness set out again to China to find a male mate for Su Lin. Instead she found two females, and brought one of them home. On February 18, 1938, she arrived at the Brookfield Zoo with a second living giant panda, Diana, later renamed Mei-Mei.

Su Lin's weight had shot up from 14 pounds (6.3 kilograms) to more than 100 (45 kilograms), and she dwarfed the new arrival. It was hoped that when Diana caught up with her they would become company for one another. Unfortunately, Su Lin died six weeks later, from a piece of wood that had become lodged in her throat.

As occurred from time to time with giant pandas in captivity, a post-mortem on Su Lin revealed that "she" was actually male. So the disappointment of losing the first giant panda was compounded by the somewhat belated fact that the zoo had possessed a potential breeding pair. But they needn't have been so disappointed, because when Diana died in 1942, it was discovered that she, too, was a he.

A third giant panda, Mei-Lan, meaning "pretty flower," was brought to the United

The full and extremely contrasting fur of the giant panda was among the reasons the animal was considered to be very pretty and quite appealing to both hunters and museum curators.

Whole communities of the bamboo plant flower and die simultaneously, and do not flower again for up to one hundred years. When the giant panda's bamboo territory becomes abnormally small, starvation can result.

The three-and-a-half-year-old male giant panda in this tree, who has spent most of his life with his mother, has now moved out on his own and is perched in a mating site, watching as a female waits for males to appear.

States by A. T. Steele, a Chicago *Daily News* correspondent, who had reported that giant pandas were actually quite plentiful and zoos were being fooled into paying great sums of money for them unnecessarily.

Mei-Lan made a stopover in Hollywood, where the two-month-old cub (which turned out to be male) actually attended a garden party on the lawn of the Hotel Ambassador. It reached the Brookfield Zoo on November 16, 1939, and went on to break early records for giant panda longevity. On September 5, 1953, it died at age fifteen.

Pandee and Pandah

During this period, both New York and St. Louis acquired giant pandas. Pandee and Pandah entered the Bronx Zoo on December 30, 1941, a gift from China to America. Pandee died after nearly four years of intestinal trouble, but Pandah lived until October 31, 1951. St. Louis acquired a male named Happy and a female named Pao-Pei. Happy lived another seven years, and Pao-Pei twelve years and nine months. Giant pandas were also acquired for zoos in London and Germany.

This high-altitude giant panda has apparently found something on a tree to tempt its taste buds. When bamboo is scarce, pandas will eat gentians, irises, crocuses, fish, eggs, honey, and chicken, and occasionally small rodents, when available.

Apparently upset at being disturbed in its mountain paradise, this giant panda is probably producing one of several sounds of which it is capable—bleating, chirping, huffing, snorting, and even "barking" when unnerved.

33

By 1963, on September 9, a female giant panda in Peking named Li Li gave birth to Ming-Ming, the first captive-born giant panda. Almost exactly a year later, on September 4, 1964, Li Li produced a second infant, Lin-Lin. It wasn't until 1980 that the first giant panda birth outside China occurred, at the Mexico City Zoo.

In April of 1972, the Chinese government sent two pandas, a male and a female, to the National Zoo in Washington, D.C., where they became perhaps the most well-known giant pandas in North America. Ling-Ling, age three, and her prospective mate, Hsing-Hsing, two, were a gift from the People's Republic of China to the people of the United States, presented to President Richard M. Nixon as a gesture of amity and goodwill when he visited China that year.

Visitors stood in line for hours waiting to spend just a minute in front of their cage. The two giant pandas did not hit it off too well, but they did manage to produce five full-term giant panda cubs, all of which died shortly after birth because of abnormal immune systems.

Ling-Ling died of heart failure December 30, 1992, at twenty-three, a venerable age for a giant panda. But she may still live on in the laboratory, because during an autopsy of her body officials extracted one hundred or so eggs they hope to fertilize and implant in a surrogate giant panda mother. At the time this book was written, Hsing-Hsing remained at the National Zoo, the only resident giant panda in the United States.

Feeding mainly on bamboo shoots and roots makes the giant panda an herbivore. But because it sometimes eats small animals, it can also be called a carnivore or an omnivore.

Hunters in the early part of this century eventually learned that it was to their advantage to look in trees for giant pandas, rather than on the ground, where they were camouflaged by jungles of bamboo and rhododendron.

AN ENDANGERED SPECIES

Asia was once the range for countless species of wildlife, including some found only on that continent. Now many of those species, including the giant panda, have been drastically reduced in numbers. Some are close to the point of extinction, including the yak, Siberian tiger, Bactrian camel, Bengal tiger, Indian leopard, Indian elephant, Indian rhinoceros, Malay tapir, gibbon, and orangutan.

At one time the giant panda could be found in much of southern and eastern China, as well as in Southeast Asia, in what was once extensive tropical rain forest. The giant panda usually lives alone in the dense bamboo and coniferous forests on the mountains, at altitudes of 5,000 to 12,000 feet (1,525 to 3,660 meters). The climate is cool and seldom goes above 15° F. (-9.4 C.) in winter, and the area, covered with clouds most of the year, is plagued by heavy rain and mist.

The giant panda was protected over most of the past two thousand years of man cultivating the mountain slopes because of the harsh climate at such high altitude. People, for the most part, encroached on the warm temperate and subtropical lower areas and left the giant panda to its temperate and cold-temperate forest climate higher up.

Although eating bamboo takes a lot of time, it does not really take much energy. Lying down is just one of the relaxed positions in which a giant panda can partake of this staple food.

Holding this shoot of bamboo in both front paws, a giant panda sits upright in a position reminiscent of a flautist making beautiful music on an (edible) instrument.

There seems to be plenty of bamboo to go around for this giant panda, one of 250 in the vast Wolong Nature Reserve, surrounded by the Qionglai Mountains in Sichuan Province.

Deforestation

Unfortunately, in this century radical deforestation prompted by the needs of China's one billion inhabitants has begun to deprive the giant panda of its last natural habitat. Increasing development for human use has driven the giant panda from its home in the fertile land of the lower mountains of southern China into the deep valleys of the eastern skirt of the Qinghai-Tibet plateau.

The forest area is rapidly disappearing because of logging operations, population growth, and agricultural expansion. Barely twelve percent of China's land remains as forest, the lowest proportion of any major country in the world.

Today the giant panda exists in the wild only in the mountains of central China in small isolated areas of the north and central portions of the Sichuan Province, in the mountains bordering the southernmost part of Gansu Province, and in the Qinling Mountains of Shaanxi Province. A recent accounting shows that there are giant pandas in six locations within these areas, resulting in a combined area of 11,088 square miles (28,725 square kilometers).

The largest area, at recent count, had some 350 giant pandas spread out over 5,134 square miles (13,270 square kilometers) of slopes on the Minshan Mountains on the border of Gansu and Sichuan provinces. About 250 giant pandas were accommodated in more than 4,025 square miles (10,425 square kilometers) in the Wolong Nature Reserve, surrounded by the Qionglai Mountains in Sichuan Province. And approximately one

The side of this mountain in Wolong is an example of the massive deforestation that has occurred in China over the years. When the forest disappears, so does food and habitat for the giant panda and other animals.

The mountains provide a majestic backdrop to this house and gardens in the Wolong Nature Reserve in China, established in 1980 as a giant panda studies center.

Although it likes to be high up in the treetops the giant panda does not enjoy being this far out in the open. It was probably forced to go that far because of some perceived or real threat in the area.

For the giant panda, the definition of casual dining is leaning lazily against a tree, gently pulling a shoot of bamboo over to its mouth before it even takes the stalk out of the ground.

This tree does not look like any challenge at all. The giant panda just wraps its "arms" and legs around the trunk and prepares to shinny its way up.

hundred were roaming an area of 1,158 square miles (3,000 square kilometers) at the southern limit of the giant panda's area, along the three mountain chains of Daxiangling, Xiaoxiangling, and Daliangshan.

Besides the extreme habitat encroachment and destruction, the giant panda is endangered by its own low reproduction rates, and by the intermittent growing habits of the bamboo plant, which is the main ingredient in its daily diet.

A female giant panda can conceive only two or three days a year. Because it takes at least eighteen months to rear her offspring, she will reproduce only once every two years. Also, there is an increasing failure to multiply because of close-kin mating within separate small groups.

As for the habits of the bamboo plant: Whole communities of the plant flower simultaneously and then promptly die. The time between the flowering of one community and the next can be as long as one hundred years. When the giant panda's bamboo territory becomes abnormally small, starvation can be the result.

The giant panda is a popular zoo animal, but has always been very difficult to keep healthy and to breed. Since there were no experts on the care and transportation of captive giant pandas, from the very beginning of the giant panda craze in the 1930s many died after their capture in China. Some died even before they left Sichuan, others on the way to their new zoo homes; many of those who did reach their destination died prematurely.

Soon it became more and more difficult to find giant pandas to replace the ones that died or to fill new requests. Eventually the Chinese began to realize that their prized animal, already rare, was near extinction. By 1949, after the establishment of the People's Republic of China, the new government moved to save all its endangered species and placed the giant panda at the top of the list.

Although the Zheng River provides water for giant pandas to drink, they are not particularly fond of immersing themselves. Instead of taking a bath they will scratch themselves or rub up against a hard surface.

Although giant pandas appear to be quite friendly, a few in zoos have been known to maul their keepers by swiping out with a paw, thrusting themselves forward or pulling a victim toward them, and then biting.

A mouthful of leaves is just the right accompaniment to whatever forest activity this giant panda is watching, from what looks like a very unstable perch high above the ground.

Protection

Currently, China is doing all it can to protect the giant panda through protection and education programs to help people realize the importance of helping these endangered animals.

Approximately twenty percent of the area where the giant panda lives has been declared reserves. In 1980, a panda studies center was established in the Wolong Nature Reserve by the World Wildlife Fund and the Chinese Ministry of Forestry. The center has conducted exhaustive studies into the life of the giant panda and worked out measures to protect it.

In 1984, scientists from Beijing University began making detailed observations in the Qinling Nature Reserve, hoping to find a way of creating an ideal forest community that would not only provide the giant panda with a habitat, but also yield more timber.

Also in 1984, the U.S. Fish and Wildlife Service listed the giant panda as an endangered species under the Endangered Species

There are probably a few giant pandas hidden on this tree-covered slope and mountainside beyond the Zheng River in Quinling, quietly munching on a mid-day meal. They peacefully go about their business all day long, trying to be as unobtrusive as possible.

This giant panda probably will not jump down and attack or perform any other sort of aggressive action. Giant pandas are quite docile and are usually perfectly content to sit in a tree and wait out any danger.

Because bamboo is so vital to a giant panda's diet, the first panda brought into the United States in 1936 was accompanied by bamboo shoot specimens which were to be used to develop a substitute food source.

Act. This means it is considered in danger of extinction throughout all or a significant portion of its range. This protection also prohibits the giant panda from being imported into the United States except under certain conditions.

The panda is still susceptible to poaching, or illegal killing, as its dense fur carries a high price in illegal markets in the Far East. The Chinese government has imposed life sentences for those convicted of poaching giant pandas. It has been reported in the past several years that China has executed men for selling skins of the endangered giant panda. In one case, two people were shot immediately after a court in Canton handed down the death sentence. One of the skins the pair sold had cost the men the equivalent of $615 U.S. It was eventually sold for nearly $24,000 in Hong Kong.

In 1980, there were about forty giant pandas in captivity in China and about thirteen in other countries. A half-dozen pairs were at various zoos in the United States for brief periods in the 1980s, but all except one have been returned to China or moved elsewhere. The giant panda became so popular among zookeepers in the 1980s that at one time more than thirty zoos and other organizations in the United States were reportedly negotiating with the Chinese to get breeding pairs.

The giant panda is also protected under the Federal Endangered Species Act and by the Convention on International Trade in Endangered Species of Wild Fauna and Flora (CITES), a treaty among more than 120 nations aimed at controlling illegal trade in endangered animal and plant species. The U.S. Fish and Wildlife Service is the federal agency responsible for the American government's compliance with CITES.

In 1993, the U.S. Department of the Interior imposed an import ban on the giant panda, after concern was raised that its survival in the wild in China was being jeopardized.

The San Diego Zoo had an import permit application on file when the ban was passed. The zoo had hoped to bring Shi Shi, a male, and Shun Shun, a female, to San Diego for at least three years. Both giant pandas were captured in March 1992, reportedly because they were seriously injured or ill.

In exchange for the giant pandas, the zoo was to pay the Chinese government $1 million a year, which would have gone toward preserving areas where the giant panda lives. At the time the permit was denied, the zoo was reportedly using its new (at the time) million-dollar giant panda home to exhibit only stuffed giant pandas.

Following the giant panda's seemingly haphazard course—recording and studying where it lives and roams in Qinling—requires the use of a collar tracking device like this one being installed on a sedated giant panda.

Enjoying hilarious sights such as this—a giant panda snoozing in a precarious position in a tree—is one of the side benefits for the researchers who study the giant panda in Qinling.

GIANT PANDA BEHAVIOR

Although its habitat has shrunk, the giant panda's habits have remained unchanged. In the wild, the giant panda spends most of its time eating, followed by periods of sleep. If the food supply in its areas is low, it has to keep moving to find enough to eat.

As it moves through the forest, the giant panda may seem to be following a haphazard course, but it actually treks higher up in the mountains during the hot summer and back down again to the lower elevations for the winter. The giant panda can become listless at temperatures above 70° F. (21 C.).

Even in extreme heat, most giant pandas are not particularly fond of water. Bathing is a very rare activity and, if a giant panda feels the need to clean itself, it might scratch with either its front or back feet, or rub its body against hard surfaces. Giant pandas in zoos have been observed refusing to immerse themselves in water. On very hot days, they might accept or play with a spray of water, or sprawl out on a block of ice. But they are not known to swim in a body of water; at the most, they will paddle at the edge.

Like many mammals the giant panda is active in the morning and again in the evening, with a sleep or rest period midday and in the middle of the night. This makes them crepuscular, as opposed to diurnal (active during the day) or nocturnal (active at night). In zoos they have been known to spend the morning patrolling, stopping occasionally for cleaning actions. Young giant pandas are much more active throughout the day than adults.

To get the bamboo to its mouth, the giant panda uses its "sixth digit," a thumb-like enlargement on one of the wrist bones. This ability allows the giant panda to sit upright and relax while it eats.

Eating and Sleeping

The giant panda spends its time wandering from one meal to the next. It feeds mainly on bamboo shoots and roots, which would make it an herbivore. But because it sometimes eats small animals, it is classed as a carnivore. Some experts, however, label it an omnivore, meaning it eats both plants and animals.

Bamboo, the only food available year-round in the giant panda's cold forests, makes up about ninety-five percent of its diet. But it offers so little nourishment that adults must eat from 20 to 80 pounds (9 to 36 kilograms), or an average of 55 pounds (25 kilograms) of shoots, stems, and leaves daily.

The giant panda in the wild also feeds on gentians, irises, crocuses, fish, and occasionally small rodents, eggs, honey, and chicken when available and if bamboo is in short supply. All that eating consumes 10 to 16 hours of the giant panda's day.

Bamboo grows in dense thickets to a height of 10 to 12 feet (3 to 3.7 meters). The giant panda prefers the younger, succulent shoots to the tougher, older stems, but to meet its needs it will devour just about all the bamboo it can get.

The lesser panda spends approximately eighty-five percent of its day eating bamboo, mostly the leaves. It also eats fruit buds, insects, larvae, mice, and bird eggs.

The giant panda seems to roam aimlessly through its territory, but it actually goes higher in the mountains during the hot summer and returns to the lower elevations for the winter season.

Are you really going to eat the whole thing? A six-foot-long (1.8-meter) shoot of bamboo is no problem for this giant panda. Nestled down in the brush, it will take no longer than a few minutes to devour the snack.

Most of a giant panda's day, from ten to sixteen hours, is consumed by searching for, chewing, and digesting approximately 55 pounds (25 kilograms) of bamboo shoots, stems, and leaves. The succulent plant makes up ninety-five percent of its diet.

Nothing could be finer than just sitting around in the sunshine, munching on a bamboo shoot. Although some giant pandas live in groups, most are quite content to spend their lives alone.

First, with its strong molars, the giant panda bites off the long stems about 8 to 16 inches (21 to 41 centimeters) above the ground, lays them down, and eats the middle part up to the beginning of the leaves. Unless it needs them, the giant panda will reject the lower, hard parts and let them lie in a pile in the jungle.

To get the bamboo to its mouth, the giant panda uses its "sixth digit," a thumb-like enlargement on one of the wrist bones. This extension is known technically as the radical sesamoid. Having this ability allows the giant panda to sit upright and back, relaxing, while it enjoys its meal.

The giant panda brings the bamboo up to its mouth, rather than lowering its mouth to the food, a movement that makes it seem very human. It then grasps the bamboo with its teeth and strips off the outer layers by turning and twisting its head. It places a peeled stalk into the corner of its mouth, crunches off a section, and then chews it with its cheek teeth. These teeth are huge, blunt, grinding stumps, so marked by ridges that drawings of them look like miniature relief maps of mountainous terrain.

After eating the giant panda will lick its front paws and forearms and wipe its face with one paw. If it has bamboo stuck in its teeth, it will pick it out with a claw. Also among its grooming rituals is the sharpening of its claws by stripping away the bark from the lower part of a tree.

The Digestive System

Even after all that, the fibers of the bamboo can be tough on the giant panda's digestive system, so the esophagus has a horny lining and the thick-walled stomach is muscular and almost gizzard-like. Surprisingly, the giant panda's intestines are only 5.5 times its overall body length, making it one of the shortest-gutted carnivores in the world.

The giant panda's digestive system is so inefficient that one would think it had only just started to evolve. Unfortunately, much of the nutrition of the swallowed bamboo is not absorbed. Giant panda droppings, which are left continually in large numbers at resting spots and on trails, are known for the large amount of undigested material they contain.

In zoos, the problem of obtaining enough bamboo to feed the day-long eaters resulted in the creation of a substitute mix of fruits, vegetables, cereals, vitamins, and minerals. Because the giant panda instinctually eats all day, zoo giant pandas would gorge them-

The giant panda's motion of bringing the bamboo up to its mouth, rather than lowering its mouth to the food, is just one of the many qualities that make it seem so human.

After eating its fill, a giant panda will look for a place to bed down, whether in a cave, a hollow tree, under a stump, under an overhanging rock, in some natural crevice, or perhaps even a tree.

selves continuously and become overweight. Thus zookeepers went back to feeding giant pandas about half their diet in bamboo shoots and stems.

After eating its fill, the giant panda will look for a place to bed down, in a cave, a hollow tree, under a stump, under an overhanging rock, in some natural crevice, or even in trees. Its sleeping posture can vary, depending on the site, but it is known to be quite flexible in these arrangements. It is possible for the giant panda to scratch its tail with its back legs and, while sitting upright, scratch one back foot with the other back foot.

Sleeping giant pandas in zoos have been observed spread out on their front with all four legs stretched out, lying flat on their backs, sitting upright in corners, or hanging from tree branches.

If the bamboo supply is good in a particular area, it may even have a "permanent" spot to which it frequently returns. This will be evident by a pile of nearby droppings and perhaps bamboo stalks broken and arranged to make a nest. A spot such as this would be where a mother would give birth to and raise her young.

With its strong molars, the giant panda first bites off the long bamboo stems about 8 to 16 inches (21 to 41 centimeters) above the ground, lays them down, and eats the middle part up to the beginning of the leaves. Unless it needs them, it will reject the lower, hard part.

Many new researchers have been surprised at the color of giant pandas, which is black and off-white or yellowish-brown because of the dirt on its fur. The litter on the back of this giant panda illustrates just how little it cares about cleanliness.

Mating and Reproduction

Ultrasound on the human fetus has become almost standard for checking the health of a baby before birth. Some parents, however, also use it to identify the gender of the impending baby. This is possible by ultrasound only if the penis of a male baby is evident—a feat not always possible, depending on his position in the uterus.

This plus-or-minus method, not via ultrasound, but by actual observation after birth, is pretty much the only way to identify the gender of a giant panda. The childlike, furry animal displays no recognizable sex characteristics outside its body except during mating, when the penis is extended, so even this method must be delayed until the panda is mature for mating. Even the testicles are so embedded in the fat of the giant panda's groin that they produce nary a bump in the body outline.

There is also no way to tell if it is a female (the minus part of the method), except during copulation, when the female generally adopts the posture of most female mammals: tail up and back arched down.

Giant panda researchers over the years have drawn or photographed the genital area of individual giant pandas whose sex they knew, to use as models to sex other giant pandas. But time and again they have failed in this regard.

Some have also claimed they could tell sex by social behavior or temperament. The female, they say, is gentler and more sociable, while the male is moody and ill-tempered. During mating, they say, males run around and bark, while females merely rub their genital areas on objects and people. But females are sometimes ill-tempered, too, and because the genital area is also home for scent glands, used to mark territory, the rubbing theory does not hold up, either.

Giant pandas of both sexes co-exist in areas several miles square. Before mating season, in the spring, usually March through May,

males expand their territories, covering the areas of several females. Some individuals have been tracked in areas up to 80 square miles (207 square kilometers).

Male giant pandas generally do not encroach on each other's territories, except during mating, but females can be combative if another female crosses onto her territory. Females with cubs, however, are generally accepted as having higher status in the jungle, and other females have been known to back off rather than confront the mother.

Females are usually ready for mating at about age five, when they begin to moan during their estrus cycle, a brief 24- to 48-hour period once a year. Her call and scent marks are often responded to by as many as three or four males. However, if the exact hour of mating has not arrived, she will run away.

When her time is right she will approach the male with her rump toward him. He will sit down propped against a tree, clasp her around the waist, and hold her tightly and let out a cry. After mating, which takes only a few minutes, she will chase him away by biting at him and find a place to sleep.

Some giant panda females in zoos have been observed to have had two heat periods a year, in fall and spring. This was characterized by the leaving of scent marks, bleating and calling, eating very little, making affectionate overtures to keepers, and pushing her genitals against their legs if they stood still

About a week after birth the cub's hair on its ears and around its eyes and shoulders begins to turn gray. Within a few weeks the fur on its legs has turned black, and the black rings around its eyes have grown larger.

Once a giant panda has exhausted the food supply in a given area, it keeps on moving throughout the forest to find another place with a more ample stock.

The mouse-sized newborn has pink skin covered with sparse white hair. It is blind and toothless, and weighs just a few ounces. It has a tail about a third of its body length, and its head is rounder and more blunt than its mother's.

within range. One giant panda, after several seasons of heat without the release of mating, developed a wicked temper.

Because a female can conceive only a few days each year, and it takes at least eighteen months to rear a cub, she will reproduce at the most every two years. With varying circumstances, she may raise four or five cubs, but only two are likely to reach adulthood.

Raising the Cub

After a 90- to 160-day gestation period, usually in August or September, the female giant panda gives birth. When she knows the time has arrived she crouches in her den and helps the baby along by pushing with her abdomen. The mouse-size newborn has pink skin covered with sparse white hair. It is blind and toothless, and weighs just a few ounces. It has a tail about a third of its body length, and its head is rounder and more blunt than the mother's.

There may be two cubs, but she may focus on one and let the other die. New research reveals that about a fourth of cubs born in the wild do not reach their first birthday.

The mother assumes total responsibility for the offspring, having chased away or ignored the father right after conception. Soon after the birth the mother picks up the cub and spends an hour or two licking it clean. She carries it in her paws or teeth, and even cradles it to her breast like we cradle human babies.

She then settles down with it to nurse. Nursing is essential, as the infant will not move on to a diet of bamboo until it is at least a year old. Newborns may need nursing

This newborn giant panda, photographed in August of 1993, is the youngest giant panda ever to be photographed in the wild, just thirty-six hours after its birth, during a moment when its mother was away from the den.

This small den beneath a rocky shelf became a sanctuary for a female giant panda when it was time for her to deliver her infant. Females usually give birth in August or September after a ninety- to one-hundred-and-sixty-day gestation period.

up to fourteen hours a day. The mother also licks the baby frequently and when it makes noises of discomfort she pats it and changes position.

For the first few days she may remain in the den with it, not leaving even to eat. Finally, after a week or more she may venture out to a nearby spot to feed. She also consumes all the infant's wastes lest they attract predators such as leopards, yellow-throated martenz, wild dogs, larger bears (territorial disputes), and possibly some large birds. A giant panda mother that notices certain threats in the vicinity may try to throw them off by going another route or even moving the den if necessary.

About a week after birth the cub's hair on its ears and around its eyes and shoulders begins to turn gray. Within a few weeks the legs turn black, and the black rings around the eyes grow larger.

By the sixteenth day the chest starts turning black, and the black circles around the eyes change into long, slanting splotches. In the next few days the neck, front, and back turn black. Within three weeks, the color spreads over the whole neck and chest, while the white hair grows longer.

By the end of the first month the cub's still-closed eyes start showing some sensitivity to light. The baby soon tries to open its eyes one at a time, for a second at a time, and over a two-week period it learns to keep them open. Vision is blurry at first, but comes into focus by three months of age.

The mother nuzzles the infant and as it gets bigger she tries to play with it, tossing it gently back and forth from one arm to the other. By the time it is three months old she may be romping with it outside, ending the session with a hug and nursing.

As the newborn ages, but before it can get around on its own, the mother panda may take it along on feeding trips. She will carry it by the nape of its neck and deposit it on the ground nearby or in a safe tree. As young giant pandas mature, their mothers sometimes leave them alone for as long as two to three days. Before this was widely known, explorers who encountered a lone giant panda baby assumed it was an orphan and "rescued" it by placing it in China's captive breeding program.

Whenever the baby makes noises of discomfort, the mother attends to it by licking, patting, or changing positions. For quite some time, the infant will be totally dependent on its mother.

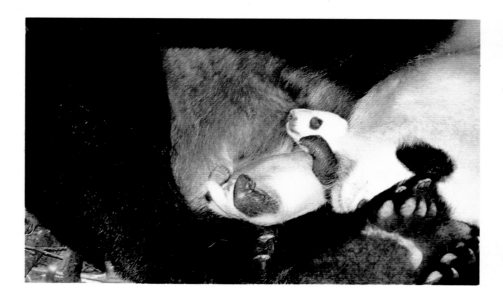

The mother giant panda begins nursing her infant almost immediately after birth, at the rate of up to fourteen hours a day. The infant is not weaned to a diet of bamboo until it is at least a year old.

After the birth the mother may stay in the den with the cub the first few days, not leaving even to eat. Finally, after a week or more she may venture out to feed nearby.

Following page: As the cub grows the mother tries to play with it, perhaps tossing it gently in her arms. By the time it is three months old she may be romping with it outside, ending the session with a hug and nursing.

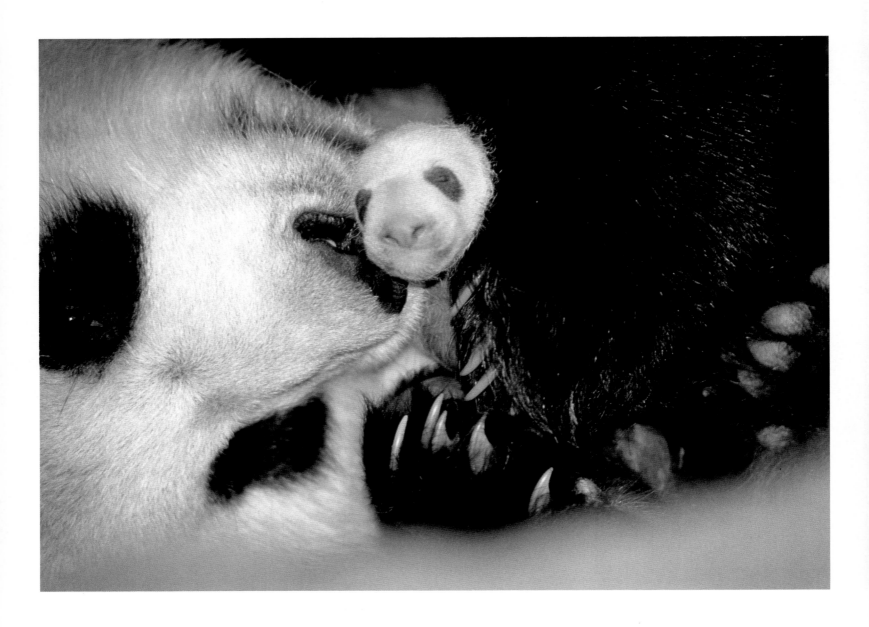

By the end of the first month the cub's eyes start showing some sensitivity to light, and over a two-week period it learns to keep them open. Vision is fully in focus by about three months.

This cub will eventually leave its mother, but some can stay up to two and a half years, usually until their mother abandons them or chases them away. At that time, the youngsters will either mark out their own solitary territory or join another group of giant pandas in the forest.

When the baby learns to crawl around, usually at three to four months, the mother will spread out additional padding, maybe pine boughs or more bamboo stems. It begins to walk on its own, and even to climb trees on its mother's back, at four to five months, when it might weigh as much as 20 pounds (9 kilograms).

One recently studied wild giant panda baby measured 28 inches long (72 centimeters) and weighed 55 pounds (25 kilograms) on its first birthday. A few weeks later he started eating bamboo. Five months later he was almost 4 feet long (1.22 meters) and weighed 110 pounds (50 kilograms). He spent less time climbing trees and more time marking tree trunks with his scent glands and sniffing at those of other giant pandas.

The baby's first milk teeth appear at two months or so, and it has nearly half its anticipated forty-two by the age of four months. It may be chewing bamboo shoots for the practice, but still the sole menu item on its diet is its mother's milk.

The baby teeth are lost at about the twelfth to fourteenth month, and soon replaced by adult teeth. There will eventually be (on each side) three upper and three lower incisors, one upper and one lower canine, four upper and four lower premolars, and two upper and three lower molars.

The infant will weigh up to 60 pounds (27 kilograms) at ten months, and about 80 pounds (36 kilograms) at one year. By the time it is eighteen months old, it will weigh about 100 pounds (45 kilograms) and be physically ready to live on its own.

As the newborn ages, but before it can get around on its own, the mother giant panda may take it along on feeding trips. She will carry it by the nape of the neck and deposit it on the ground nearby or in a safe tree, sometimes for as long as two to three days.

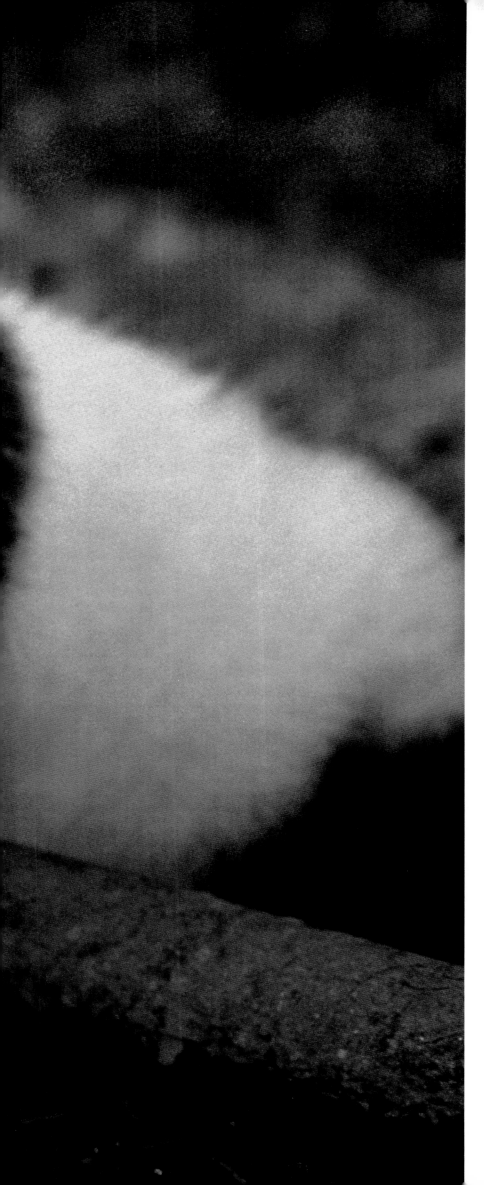

Independence

As the cub grows it learns about being independent—to approach any suspicious animal or object from downwind so it can catch a scent of it before its own presence is known, to distinguish the sounds of the forest, and to know what is and is not safe. Eventually it learns how to grapple with the bamboo, even though it may not yet be living off it, and to snare some small game, honey, or fish that crosses its path. It also spends time playing, doing impressive acrobatics and making up games for itself with nature's toys, such as ice and rocks.

The youngster might strike out on its own or it may end up that way because the mother will abandon it or chase it off. Abandonment is more likely to occur if the mother mates and becomes pregnant again. But some young giant pandas have been known to stay with their mothers much longer, perhaps up to two and a half years.

Giant pandas may end up living solitary lives or in small groups consisting of breeding males and females, their cubs, and young males. Inbreeding does occur, and can decrease reproductivity and make a population more susceptible to disease.

The young giant panda who has struck out on its own will start staking out its own territory. With current conservation actions in place, and the possibility or more to come, new giant pandas in the wilds of their native China may actually have a chance at normal,

As the cub grows it gradually becomes more and more independent, learning to approach any suspicious animal or object from downwind, so it can catch a scent of it before its own presence is known.

safe-from-man lives. Some day, perhaps, there will be enough of them again so that we can all become familiar with them at zoos or sanctuaries in our own locales.

But, although the giant panda needs our protection, it is no mere dumb animal, and has been observed, as this anecdote illustrates, to even have a little bit of spunk: One wild female giant panda that occasionally wandered into a local logging station spent some time watching the humans work the TV and videocassette recorder. After a while, when left to her own devices, she actually was observed pushing the VCR buttons with her paws, and was able to fast-forward and stop the tape.

The nineteen-month-old cub, almost as big as her mother at 120 pounds (54 kilograms), watches as her mother feeds during an outing from the den. Although the cub looks like an adult, she is apparently not ready to move out on her own.

Although the giant panda's habitat and existence have been threatened in the past, this gentle giant's future is looking up, thanks to current conservation and research efforts.

INDEX

*Page numbers in **bold-face** type indicate photo captions.*

Ailuropoda genus, 13, 21
Ailuropus genus, 21
Ailurus genus, 13, **14**, 21
anatomy of pandas, 7
  digestive system, 55–57
  sex characteristics, **23**, **27**
  sex organs, 59
  tails, **11**
  teeth, **10**
  "thumbs" of giant pandas, **11**, **14**, **49**, 55

baby pandas (cubs), 59, 60–67, **60**, **63**, **66**, **70**
  feeding of, 67
  independence for, 69–70, **69**
bamboo, 14, **31**, **34**, **37**, **38**, **41**, 45, 50–55, **52**, **57**
  alternatives to in pandas' diet, 33
  habitat of, 42
bears, 13–14
  brown bear (*Ursus arctos*), 13
  giant pandas mistaken for, 18–21
behavior
  cleaning, **42**
  of cubs, 60–67
  feeding, 50–55, **52**
  of giant pandas, **45**, 49
  independence for cubs, 69, 69–70
  reproduction and mating, 59–60
  sleep, 57
  wake-sleep cycles, **23**
  walking and climbing, 11, **13**, 67
birth of cubs, 60, **60**
Bronx Zoo (New York), 22, 28, 33
Brookfield Zoo (Chicago), 28, 31, 33
brown bear (*Ursus arctos*), **13**
brown giant pandas, **28**

captivity, giant pandas in, 22, 28–33, **28**, 46
  diet of, 55–57
  reproduction in, 34
China
  deforestation in, 38–42, **38**
  evolution of pandas in, 17
  pandas as endangered species in, 37
  pandas "discovered" in, **17**, 18–21, **18**
  pandas sent to U.S. by, 33, 34
  protection for giant pandas in, 45–46
  reduction of panda habitat in, **21**
cleaning behavior, **42**, 49
climbing, **7**, 11
coat
  of cubs, 63
  of giant pandas, 7, **31**
  of lesser pandas, 14
coloration of pandas, 7, 13, **57**
  of cubs, 63
Convention on International Trade in
    Endangered Species of Wild Fauna and
    Flora (CITES), 46
cubs, *see* baby pandas

David, Père Armand, 18–21, **18**
deforestation, 38–42, **38**
Diana (Mei-Mei, panda), 31
diet of giant pandas, 33, 34, 45, 50
  in captivity, 55–57
  of cubs, 67
digestive system, 55–57
"discovery" of pandas, **17**, 18–21, **18**

eating, *see* feeding
endangered species, 37
  giant pandas as, 45–46
Endangered Species Act (U.S.), 45–46
evolution of pandas, 17, **18**
eyes of pandas, 7, **63**, **66**

feeding, 50–55
  on bamboo, **31**, **34**, **37**, **38**, **41**, 45, **52**, **57**
  of cubs, 67, **67**
  diet for, 33
  by lesser pandas, 50
  nursing of cubs, 60–63, **63**
  teeth for, **10**
  "thumbs" used in, **49**
female giant pandas, 59–60
  birth of cubs to, 60, **60**
  cubs cared for by, **67**, 69
  nursing of cubs by, **63**
  reproduction in, 42
Fish and Wildlife Service, U.S., 45, 46
fur, *see* coat

giant panda (*Ailuropoda melanoleuca*), **4**, 7
  behavior of, 49, **50**
  brown, **28**
  in captivity, 22, 28–33, **28**
  cubs, 59
  currently endangered, 37
  deforestation of habitat of, 38–42, **38**
  diet of, **33**, 34
  "discovery" of, 18–21, **18**
  docile behavior of, 45
  feeding on bamboo, **37**, **41**, **52**
  habitat and history of, 17
  habitat of, **41**
  low reproduction rates of, 42
  protection for, 45–46
  in Qinling Nature Reserve, **46**
  range and history of, 17
  reproduction of, 59–60
  reproduction of, in captivity, 34
  sex characteristics of, **23**, **27**
  size of, 7, **10**
  "thumbs" of, **11**, 14, **49**, 55
  walk of, **13**
  in zoos, 42

habitat of pandas, 17, **17**, 37, **41**
  deforestation of, 38–42, **38**
  reduction in, **21**
Happy (panda), 33
Harkness, Ruth, 22, 28, 31
Harkness, William Harvest, Jr., 22
hibernation, 14
Hsing-Hsing (panda), **4**, 34
humans
  appeal of pandas to, 4, 7
  deforestation by, 38–42, **38**
  pandas hunted by, 21, **21**, 23, 34
hunting of pandas, 21, **21**, 23, 34
  current, 46

independence for cubs, 69–70, **69**
Interior, U.S. Department of, 46

lesser panda (*Ailurus fulgens*), 14
  "discovery" of, 21
  face of, **14**
  feeding by, 50
  as member of racoon family, 13
  size of, **10**
  tails of, 11
Li Li (panda), 34
Ling-Ling (panda), 34
Lin-Lin (panda), 34

male giant pandas, 59
mating, 59–60
Mei-Lan (panda), 31–33
Mei-Mei (Diana, panda), 31
Mexico City Zoo, 34
Milne-Edwards, Alphonse, 18–21
Ming-Ming (panda), 34

names for pandas, 21, **27**, **28**
National Zoo (Washington, D.C.), 4, 34
Nixon, Richard M., 34
nursing of cubs, 60–63, **63**

Pandah (panda), 33
pandas
  anatomy of, 7
  animals related to, 13–14
  currently endangered, 37
  deforestation of habitat of, 38–42, **38**
  "discovery" of, 18–21, **18**
  as endangered species, 3–4
  habitat and history of, 17
  hunting of, 21, **21**, 23, 34
  names for, 21, **27**, **28**
Pandee (panda), 33
Pao-Pei (panda), 33
poaching of giant pandas, 46
predators of pandas, 63

Qinling Nature Reserve (China), 45, **46**
Qionglai Mountains (China), **17**, 38, **38**

racoons, 13, **13**
red panda, *see* lesser panda (*Ailurus fulgens*)
reproduction, 59–60
  in captivity, 34
  low rates of, 42
Roosevelt, Kermit, 21, 28
Roosevelt, Theodore, 21, **21**
Roosevelt, Theodore, Jr., 21, 28

San Diego Zoo, 46
senses of pandas, 7
sex characteristics of pandas, **23**, **27**, 59
Shi Shi (panda), 46
Shun Shun (panda), 46
skulls of pandas, 7
sleep, **23**, 49, **55**, 57
Smith, William Tangier, 28
sounds produced by pandas, 11, **33**
Steele, A.T., 33
Su Lin (panda), 22, 28, 31

tails, of lesser pandas, **11**
teeth, of giant pandas, **10**, 55, 57, 67
territoriality, 59
"thumbs" of giant pandas, **11**, 14
  used in feeding, **49**, 55

United States
  giant pandas declared endangered species
    by, 45–46
  giant pandas sent by China to, 33, 34
Ursus genus (bears), 18
  see also bears

vocalications of pandas, 11, **33**

wake-sleep cycles, **23**, 49
walk of pandas, 11, **13**
  by cubs, 67
water, **42**, 49
Wolong Nature Reserve (China), **17**, 38–42, 45
  deforestation in, **38**
World Wildlife Fund, 45
wrist bones of giant pandas, 11

Young, Jack, 22
Young, Quentin, 22
young pandas, *see* baby pandas

zoos, 3
  behavior of giant pandas in, 49
  feeding of giant pandas in, 55–57
  giant pandas in, 4, **23**, 28–33, **42**, 46
  pandas reproducing in, 34